TROISIÈME VAGUE

TROISIÈME VAGUE

LUCY K SHAW

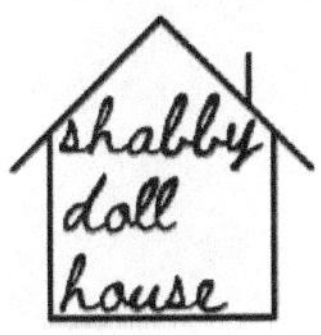

First published by Shabby Doll House
October 2021
www.shabbydollhouse.com
@shabbydollhouse

Interior design by Lucy K Shaw
Cover design by Lucy K Shaw and Jake Muilenburg
Set in Bodoni
Cover title set in Bodoni FLF

ISBN: 978-1-7379242-0-3

In memory of

Barbara Ellis

1930 - 2020

JE VEUX VIVRE AVEC TOI

A week in my life,
February 2021

Throat sore from singing Florence and the Machine songs with the acoustic guitar in the Airbnb. Slept for 9 hours in a luxurious bed. I got up and poured myself a glass of sparkling water and a glass of Granatapfel Club Maté. I guess you can get German products if you go far enough east in France.

It's sunny and five degrees (Celsius) in Lyon. I'm looking out of the window at the roof of the Hotel de Ville. There is a bright gold statue of something, glistening in the light.

I was making myself laugh by singing songs from the playlist to Chris's yoga class yesterday. He included Shake It Out, by the aforementioned Florence.

Chris said he used to listen to the album with an ex when he was in college, and I said I had listened a lot in headphones when I lived in Toronto, mostly on the subway, around the same time, when it came out.

I couldn't get through the line, *I'm always dragging that horse around* without laughing, last night.

It occurs to me now, having looked up her age, (a year older than me), that this was a funny thing for someone in their early twenties to express...

Though I guess we both related.

Chris's aforementioned ex has been on our minds this past week after they ran into each other at a virtual yoga class. Chris said he had noticed a shirtless man in little shorts at the beginning and had noted the scandalous look, but it wasn't until the end when returning to the screen in order to leave the meeting that he had realised it was someone he'd once loved.

Okay, he didn't phrase it that way. But it felt to me like the premise for a short story. I can imagine it in *The New Yorker*. Heavy on the flashbacks.

Synchronised stretching thousands of miles apart.

The first time they had been doing the same thing at the same time since Florence and the Machine came out.

Why are we in Lyon? Mostly because it's Chinese New Year.

I work for two Chinese companies, teaching English to children. And this is the one time every year when the schools close and I get a break for a few days.

It feels nice to have this uninterrupted stretch of being myself.

We're not currently under lockdown in France, and we are allowed to travel around the country, although we do have a 6pm curfew.

We took the train to Marseille first and stayed there for three nights.

We ordered tapas, Vietnamese and then Lebanese food.

We ran 10km by the sea.

And then yesterday morning we took the train to Lyon. It was Valentine's Day and we ordered pizza for dinner.

In the small city in Burgundy where we have been living during the pandemic, vegetarian options, international options, are very limited. So we wanted to take full advantage of other peoples' cooking while in the big cities.

This is my first time in Lyon and I find myself doing something I dislike, which is trying to describe the place to myself in terms of other places I've been before. There is a distinctly central European feeling to the architecture, to the landscape and even to the people, which makes sense, of course, based on where it is... but trying to patch together an identity for a place based on things I already know feels reductive. Albeit inevitable until I come up with a new system.

I'm going to go for a run now.

Running in a new city is my favourite way to see somewhere.

Travel runs, I call them...

In 2019 I wrote a running diary of all the places I ran that year. Lisbon, Berlin, New York, Valencia, Prague, Paris, Santorini, Yorkshire, Athens, etc.

Chris didn't run at that point, so I would go off by myself and explore.

When I think of those experiences now, I wonder if that was when I was *most myself*.

Or if that's just how I'd like to be remembered.

He started joining me in the first lockdown when he couldn't go to yoga classes in person anymore. So now the travel runs can be longer. It's a couple of days later, by the way, and I'm back *home* in Nevers. It's nearly 9am and I'm waiting for a fresh batch of maté to boil, lying under a blanket in pyjamas. I wanted to read some more of *The Freezer Door*, a book that I gave Chris for Christmas, but he has been reading it too, and I think it was on his bedside table, and I didn't want to wake him up as I slipped away. So here I am, writing.

I was thinking about you on our run. That's how I decided who to write this to. I thought, what am I doing? And who do I want to tell about it?

I decided it was whoever I thought about while I was running along the Rhone.

We ended up running 15km around Lyon that day. Up to the basilica and looking out over the city to the mountains. Down through the gardens, through the old town, along the Saône edge of the Presqu'ile to the confluence of the two rivers and back along the Rhone. I don't usually run that far. 10km has been the upper limit of my imagination. But now having gone further, I feel like I could go further still.

Why not?

I have also been reading *The Years* by Annie Ernaux. The English translation. It's so good. I keep thinking about this one part where she refers to her older relatives, and their fixation with the wars, how that was all anybody wanted to talk about during family meals:

'But they only spoke of what they had seen and could re-live while eating and drinking. They lacked the talent and conviction to speak of things they'd been aware of but had not seen.'

It was fun to have a guitar for a few days in Lyon. I have been thinking about buying one for a while now. It's strange because there were years when I couldn't have been without one… What would I have done with my hands? But I think, honestly, now, I'm a little scared of that person. The intensity of her. I can see myself sitting for hours singing the same things over and over and I associate it with somewhere I can't afford to go anymore.

But it's just some wood and strings.

Isn't it?

Maybe I can handle it.

9:51am, I just checked the news for the first time today. Nothing has changed. I have to go teach soon. And then the hours will pass and I will come back to me later.

22

In the shower I started thinking about what I said before about that seeing-an-ex-at-an-online-yoga-class story. I imagined writing the story in secret, because Chris had alluded to putting it in a poem and *it's not my story to tell.* But for some reason, convinced by the marketability of the subject matter, perhaps, finding myself compelled to risk everything and write it anyway. This would never happen. But in the story of the story, I'd start out trying to fictionalise the characters and the details, before eventually just thinking, fuck it - it's already perfect - and dropping the veil.

The story would be published in *The New Yorker* under a fake name and I would get away with it for a time because Chris would never read *The New Yorker*. But then some months later, I would get caught in either one of two ways: Either I'd have too much money and he would want to know how I could suddenly afford such an expensive guitar. Or when he finally published his poem, someone would send him a link like, *omg this reminded me of an incredible story I read...*

Another day passed. I can feel the vacation being sucked out of me. I have seven classes to teach today.

I feel so up and down and out of sync sometimes. All of a sudden, it's like I go out of tune. And then I say, *why?* And that's the dumbest question.

I run by the Loire and listen to *Pink Friday* by Nicki Minaj.

Few things move me more than the following lyrics:

I ain't gotta get a plaque
I ain't gotta get awards
I just walk up out the door
All the girls will applaud
All the girls will commend
As long as they understand
That I'm fighting for the girls
That never thought they could win
'Cause before they could begin
You told 'em it was the end
But I am here to reverse
The curse that they live in

I stop for a few seconds and watch two coypus swimming to, and then sitting on a branch that has fallen by the riverbank.

Coypus look like beavers except their tails look more like rats'.

As I turn to start again, I realise a woman passing by is saying something to me, presumably about the animals.

I can only hear Nicki Minaj.

I smile in agreement and run away.

I build a chest of drawers we had delivered from IKEA and paint the river onto it.

The colours I use are called Granada, Santa Fe, and Menton.

I did have a great moment in my classes, yesterday.

Now I'm writing this the following morning. And I want to tell you about my favourite student, Alina.

I have been teaching her since she was six years old, and today is her ninth birthday!

I hadn't seen her for a week and a half because of Chinese New Year. Usually we have class every Tuesday and Friday.

When I logged into the classroom, I held up a card to the camera with a photo of a hamster on it, and I saw her face explode into an enormous smile. She said hello to the hamster and then I opened the card and showed her the message inside: *To Alina, Happy Birthday, Love from Lucy.*

She gasped.

It was so cute. And then I sang happy birthday to her and drew her a cake. And we somehow sustained the high for the entire class. It was so much fun. It makes me feel a little glowy to think about.

When we first met, she was so shy, she would literally whisper. It was so difficult to communicate with her. But over the past two and a half years, she has become so confident and funny. It is amazing to watch her grow up and find the words to express herself.

I think of this as an important relationship in my life.

It's nearly midnight on Saturday now. When did I start writing this? Monday morning. It feels like so much has happened. And actually, nothing has happened, but there is so much I haven't mentioned.

I'm finding it very difficult to talk to people, I notice. Or I just don't want to do it. If there's no premise, like a book club or a writing project, I don't want to face a conversation. I sent my grandma flowers instead of calling. I awkwardly struggled through a group dinner on zoom, kept saying the wrong things. I think about making plans with people and then I can't think of anything worse.

I have been 'hosting' the yoga classes Chris teaches on zoom. Which means that I let people in from the waiting room, mute them once the class starts, check the sound is okay, etc.

Then my computer displays all these people, some of whom I know, moving around in their bedrooms for an hour. And I just fold some laundry or write a little.

It's not something I would have predicted happening to me.

31

But I guess I accept my fate.

The weather has suddenly turned to spring. It was nineteen degrees this afternoon. I heard that there is dust in the air, blown up from the Sahara.

I woke up and decided to go running. I did another 5km by the Loire. It was one of those where you barely remember it happened. Over so quickly. I was listening to the audiobook of *Remembrance of Things Past* and when I came back Chris was still in bed and I made him laugh doing my impression of Proust, which felt nice.

I taught a couple of classes and reorganised the closet and then we went for a bike ride. We cycled to a nearby village and found a 14th century castle.

I told Chris that I noticed I have been avoiding talking to people and he suggested that maybe I'm depressed. But I told him that I don't feel depressed. I feel fine, going for runs, reading books, teaching classes, doing my little tasks, trying to pass the time... what feels depressing is talking to other people about how miserable things are.

He didn't seem convinced at the time. But then the next day he saw a meme about it.

Chris went to another yoga class when we got home. I swear that's his whole life now.

I had been planning on completing the closet reorganisation but then he was stretching in the bedroom, in front of the closet, so I decided to call Grandma. She said she was eating her dinner, so I wrote a little more of this and she called me back soon after.

She's doing pretty well, considering.

I speak to her more now than I did before the pandemic. We gave her an iPad during the first lockdown, so now we can FaceTime. She can hear a lot better with headphones in than she can using the extra-loud-large-buttoned-elderly-people-phone that's supposed to help her.

She told me about how various members of her family died. Her aunt (aneurysm), her older brother (asbestosis), her younger brother (mysteriously in the Philippines), her mum (just laid down and said, 'I'm dying, Arthur.')

She said that the flowers I sent are still doing well.

She said that she has changed the water twice.

Every second Sunday I host the ~Profound Experience of Poetry Book Club, which reminds me of who I think I really am.

This week we were talking about *How to Wash a Heart* by Bhanu Kapil.

I read it first on the train back from Lyon, and then again in the couple of hours before the meeting.

Before we started, I felt subdued and detached.

But by the end, I felt regenerated.

I danced around the living room afterwards.

It's Monday again now so I will stop writing and my life will continue in hopefully much the same way. But I want to tell you one more thing.

When we were on the train to Marseille, it was one of the happiest times I've had recently. As you go so far south in France, into Provence, the landscape suddenly changes. Cypress and olive trees emerge. The sky is bigger. Bluer. Flat plains surrounded by imposing mountains tell you that you're entering another phase of the earth.

I used to have this experience all the time.

For years we lived in such a way that we could travel almost constantly. The world felt relational and accessible. I expected life to look and feel differently at any given moment. But lately it has felt as though everything ends at the horizon.

On that train ride, I was reminded of how it felt when we lived in Aix-en-Provence for a few months, a few years ago. The brightly coloured vegetables and flowers we would buy from the morning market. The way the sunlight would hit the windowsill where we would sit and eat gazpacho at lunchtime. The crisp air at the top of Mont Sainte-Victoire, and the views over the same countryside that captivated Paul Cézanne. The taste of rosé on a terrasse, with someone smoking over your shoulder.

As the train pulled into the city and the Mediterranean suddenly came into view, I gasped. Just like Alina did.

I felt so overwhelmed.

Happy Chinese New Year.

I miss you!

JE NE SUIS PAS SEUL, IL Y A LES MOTS

Another week in my life,
March 2021

I'm going to start writing again. I feel strange. It's 12:31am and Chris is in the living room, translating. I'm in bed.

42

Today my sister texted me, *Do you know a Jamie Cooper?* *lol, yeah,* I responded, *from school.*

I thought about Jamie Cooper for the first time in a long time. The most popular girl in my secondary school. Coops, some people called her. She was beautiful with olive skin and blonde highlights, the high priestess of the coolest girls, the desired object of all the sportiest boys, but against all odds, somehow, not a bitch. She would remember people's names and say *Hiya* when she passed you in the corridor. I remember her denim jacket and the way she wore her oversized shirt tucked into tight, fitted and slightly flared polyester trousers.

I can't remember what shoes she wore during the school day but I remember that once the bell rang, she and all of her disciples would slip into their trainers in order to walk out of the school gates, always carrying a plastic shopping bag containing their P.E kit and folders in addition to their matching draw-string duffles.

I thought my sister was going to tell me that she was working at the same school as her. Kate has been doing a teacher-training course in our hometown to pass the pandemic.

Anyway, *she died,* is what she wrote next.

Oh my god, what?

I searched for Jamie Cooper on Facebook and quickly found out that she had two daughters, about eight and six, no mention of a partner. She seems to have been ill before, had some kind of organ transplant. I don't know how she died (or lived) or anything about what happened. She's just... dead, suddenly. To me. I haven't thought about her in a long time. Haven't seen her in fifteen years, probably.

Never would have seen her again, I imagine, no matter how long we'd both have lived.

I dreamed about both of the dead girls last night.

The other one is in the news. I didn't know her either. But she was from the same city as me, York. And she was also the same age as me, 33. Her name was Sarah Everard. She was walking home last week in London and then yesterday the police found 'human remains' in some woods in Kent. Then they arrested another policeman on suspicion of murder.

When you google *Jamie Cooper*, the first results are for a 16-year-old cheerleader from Georgia who died from a drug overdose last month in the apartment of a 25-year-old man.

I tried not to let their deaths affect me. Because I didn't know the girls. Because it's easier not to think about them. Because there is enough to worry about, all of the time.

But my sister and my mum told me they felt upset last night.

Then I started to feel it too.

I told Chris about them at dinner and described what I had learned on Facebook. It seemed like Jamie Coops loved being alive, like she loved being with her two daughters, that she had been a very happy person.

'Really makes the case against the existence of a benevolent god,' Chris said, which made me feel like we may never really understand each other.

I pulled a face.

I dreamed about Marie-Soleil too. My best friend from university. We haven't spoken in forever. She dropped off the face of the earth/internet a long time ago.

In the dream, we met in the library in Montréal and walked up the mountain, then later we were in Paris, in a place that doesn't exist in Paris. She was impressed by how much my French has improved. In the dream, my French was really good.

I woke up feeling glad I had spent time with her.

A list of things that make me feel good about myself
lately:

-Remembering to buy household supplies such as dish
soap, foil, trash bags, etc before they run out.
-Cleaning the bathroom.
-Taking out the recycling.

Yesterday afternoon, Chris and I ran a loop that we'd only done once before. The other way up the river. It's not as beautiful but I was relieved to sacrifice beauty for something different. Up and down a lot of small hills. The sky was grey, thick with clouds, and we started talking about who would potentially care for our non-existent offspring in the event of our tragic, untimely deaths.

Nobody seemed particularly appropriate or qualified.

(No offense.)

This was a sort of follow-up to a conversation we'd had a few days ago in which I said I don't really feel like I want any children at the moment, but maybe it is something we have to actually think about soon, seeing as time continues to pass.

It doesn't feel palatable, what I have written so far.

Now it's 12:48am, another day, and I'm almost ready for bed. The last time I wrote to you, it was just after my period had finished, or in other words, the happiest time of my month.

This time I started writing in the build-up. And here I am now, in the middle.

The complete lack of activity in my life makes my menstrual cycle feel more pronounced. I'm so aware of it. Can feel it carving its way through time like a river. There's no way to be distracted from the agonising pain and the dull passing of hours when nothing ever happens except death in the distance.

And sometimes a new podcast.

You can probably tell, reading this, that I haven't seen anyone I know in months. I haven't seen a friend since last summer. But I've been listening to the audiobook of *Remembrance of Things Past.* And I spent most of last week alone, listening to Alice Notley interviews. I'm trying to get into the zone to write something.

My thoughts are more jumbled than last month, though.

As I was brushing my teeth, I became involved in an in-depth internal monologue about daffodils, which I bought this morning at the market for the first time this year. (The people who run the flower stand are a couple, probably 10 years older than us. They always make a point of calling us *les jeunes* and giving us a free rose.) We buy a lot of flowers to make ourselves feel better.

I painted some daffodils last weekend. I made a card for my mum, because it's Mother's Day (in England) tomorrow. And already, today, she sent me a photo of the painting in a frame on her mantelpiece.

I take the ability to make something beautiful for granted, but I am pleased with myself for having the competence to put it in the mail.

Her first Mother's Day without a mother.

I don't even know the French word for daffodils.

I know the German word, *Narzissen*.

In York, there is a medieval tower on a grassy hill in the centre of the city. Every spring the hill blooms into a sea of daffodils. We must have all seen this, growing up. Me and Sarah and Jamie.

I can't believe I am writing all of this about flowers.

But really it's about my nana. She died last April. Six days before her ninetieth birthday.

She was diagnosed with metastatic cancer and they told us that she had weeks or months left to live. But then, suddenly, it seemed like days, and I rushed back to England. This was in late January. And we spent the next two months visiting her, first in the hospital and then in the care home, before we all got locked down.

It was a privilege to spend that time with her. Really it was. We brushed her hair and moisturised her hands, listened to her stories. I remember saying to my mum that Nana would never see daffodils again. I always associated them with her. April birthday. A sign that good times were coming.

But she did hold on long enough. We filled her room with them, and she loved it.

What must it have been like for her when the visits
stopped though?

She didn't understand.

She asked us if there was a war.

It feels like so long ago.

This time last year, I was visiting her almost every day. And then the lockdown happened, and we never saw her again, until the funeral.

10 people, outside, for 15 minutes.

This is the kind of thing that people are talking about when they tweet about collective trauma and how we are yet to even begin processing what has happened to us, I imagine.

My nana deserved a proper funeral.

Sarah Everard deserves a proper funeral.

Jamie Cooper deserves a proper funeral.

To type those sentences feels cataclysmic.

63

Saturday morning. Church bells ringing for 10 o'clock.

I start teaching at 11.

I have been teaching seven days a week for the past few months because it feels like there is no point in taking breaks. What else am I going to do?

I'm going to need extra money when we can hang out with people again, so that I can buy things that I don't really want.

I get up before Chris and sit on the sofa and read something or write something. I finish *The Years* by Annie Ernaux, and *The Descent of Alette* by Alice Notley and *Greyhound* by Aeon Ginsberg. I flick through a book of David Hockney sketches for inspiration. I slowly work my way through *The Freezer Door* by Mattilda Bernstein Sycamore. I paw at *The Cipher* by Molly Brodak but can't bring myself to open it.

Another dead woman I didn't know.

I listen to the audiobook of *Tribe* by Sebastian Junger, some nonfiction book about veterans reintegrating back into society after combat.

On Sunday mornings, loud African church music pours out of the disused pharmacie opposite our building. Live music. Religious services are one of the only things still allowed to happen. They have someone drumming and someone playing an electric organ. Many, many people inside singing, screaming hallelujah. If we have the windows open, it's like we're in there.

But I close them so I can teach my students.

I enter my little portal to China.

Sky tells me his teacher caught a boy and a girl kissing at school this week. He's 13. He says he doesn't have a girlfriend yet, but 'I want.'

I tell him to expect that romantic relationships may reconfigure frequently in the coming years.

He draws a diagram of several stick figures and draws arrows between them. Maybe this boy like this girl but this girl like this boy and this other boy like this girl too?

Yeah, exactly, I say.

And what if... can this boy like this one? He says, pointing to one of the male stick figures. Testing the waters.

Oh yeah, definitely, I tell him. That will happen too.

Grace tells me that she and her best friend Star are tutoring their other friend Elsa, because Elsa is falling behind and they can't let that happen.

Alina says she already knows the story of Little Red Riding Hood and it's too scary. She wants to talk about cakes today, for some reason.

Lydia is in a restaurant with her entire family, eating hotpot.

She says it is very yummy.

Barbie has a new short haircut and looks really cool.

I say, *you look fourteen!* (She's twelve.)

Eden is in a bad mood but doesn't want to tell me why. *No why!!!*

Amy introduces me to her pet moths which she found in her family's sack of rice and relocated to a plastic bag. I ask if they have names.

She says she hasn't asked them.

Chris has a big deadline tomorrow. He needs to translate about seven thousand more words of an eighteen-thousand-word document he has been working on over the past few days.

When it goes like this, I take on all the other tasks required for two people to live comfortably.

This often used to include packing both of our suitcases and figuring out how to get from one place to the next. But more recently it just means cooking and washing dishes again and again.

We operate symbiotically, moving around our small apartment like pieces on a chess board.

Or at least, it feels that way to me.

I have no idea how to play chess.

Some family friends in Paris ask if we could cat-sit for them for the month of April.

They are in their late sixties so I presume from their willingness to travel that they must have both been vaccinated. And they are dual citizens of France and the US so I presume, also, that they must have decided to go over there where there are less rules to follow.

We say okay, why not. A change of scenery would be nice. Although there have been rumours of a possible lockdown for the Île de France region only, so far it hasn't happened. It would be annoying if we went there and then got put in confinement again.

Imagine us trying to escape from Paris with the cat.

For context, and for myself in the future:

The second confinement ran from October 31st until December 15th. During that time we were only allowed out for essential purposes such as buying food or exercise. We had to sign an attestation form every time we went outside, which was tedious.

Then when the confinement ostensibly ended, we began an 8pm curfew for a couple of weeks over the Christmas and New Year period.

Cases rose, obviously, over the holidays, and the 8pm curfew quickly changed to 6pm, so we haven't been outside past six o'clock since January 2nd.

It is now March 14th and there is no clear indication from the government about when things could possibly change.

Restaurants, bars, museums etc, have all been closed since the end of October.

And cases are still rising.

At the beginning of the year, it wasn't as frustrating. It was dark by 5pm and it was cold, and there was nowhere to go. But now it's light past 7 o'clock. Some days it is even warm. In a couple of weeks when the clocks change, it won't get dark until after 8pm.

And now everyone I know in America is getting vaccinated.

And we are still months away.

Another night up past midnight writing in this document.

I feel melancholy. And also distracted by all of the voices I have been reading. I feel noisy.

I had to take a break from running for a few days because my knees started to ache. I don't know why. It has never happened to me before.

I lie on the bed with them elevated on pillows. I ice them. I cannot afford to be injured.

Running is one of the only things I have left!

Chris has just finished translating the thing that he has been working on for the past few days. It was horrible. I proofread it this afternoon. Something about the links between healthcare and the environment in Switzerland. It took me two hours just to read it, so I can only imagine how he feels now.

I made a point of asking how much he'll get paid for it to try to make him feel better. And now we are listening to gentle spa music and waiting for a mediocre pizza to arrive.

I just had a strange experience.

Chris answered the phone, *Vous êtes ici? Cool. J'arrive.*

And he hadn't showered yet (he was intending to shower), so I said, *I'll go!*

Put my shoes on and ran down the stairs.

I walked into the hall and the automatic light didn't come on for a few seconds. My body just froze in the dark thinking of what happened to Sarah Everard. What happened to her! The light flickered on. I took a deep breath and walked a few paces to the front door of the building. It's one of those large, old, wooden doors that a horse and carriage could have passed through. I opened it up and the delivery man was right there in front of the door with the boxes. I kind of stumbled, like *uuhhhmm merci!* Suddenly felt gripped with fear of being in the dark at my front door with this stranger. He just passed me the pizza, nothing happened. I closed the door and went inside.

I feel ridiculous.

The French word for daffodil is *jonquille*.

Mes jonquilles sont mortes après quelques jours.

I speak to my grandma on FaceTime. She has just been for her second dose. She says she doesn't think the nurse actually injected her. She didn't feel a thing. But she's going to wait until tomorrow before she does something about it, because she usually feels achy the day after a vaccination and she's hoping that she's wrong.

I don't know what to think.

She says she has a hair appointment booked for the first day hairdressers are scheduled to reopen, and she's thinking of trying a new style. (She has had the same haircut for my entire life.)

She asks me if I know that Ursula Von Something woman?

I say, *the head of the European Commission?*

She says, yes, she thinks that she has lovely hair, and she'd like to try something like that.

It's Thursday again. I think I've been writing for a week.

It's past midnight again. Things continue to get worse.

There was a mass-shooting at a spa in Atlanta yesterday.

Six Asian-American women were murdered.

I am so low on energy.

How many dead women have I written about?

Do men die?

Jamie Cooper is dead.
Another Jamie Cooper is dead.
Sarah Everard is dead.
Molly Brodak is dead.
Barbara Ellis, my nana, is dead.
Soon Chung Park is dead.
Hyun Jung Grant is dead.
Suncha Kim is dead.
Yong Ae Yue is dead.
Xiaojie Tan is dead.
Daoyou Feng is dead.

I can type this and I can say it quietly out loud. But I don't believe I really understand it. Everyone feels too far away.

How about some men die for a change!!! I write to Sarah Jean.

That's what I'm saying!!! She writes back.

Castex, the prime minister, announces a new four week lockdown.

No travel permitted. It starts tomorrow.

I wonder what will happen to the cat.

STRAIGHT OUTTA COMBRAY

A Nothing Week,
April 2021

As I was falling asleep last night, I was trying to remember all of the places we went and all of the people we had seen by this stage of the year, two years ago. 2019.

On one of the first days of January, we flew to Barcelona, spent a few days with Andrew, who came from Toronto, hung out with Luna and Antonio and Ulises, got really into vermut and Rosalia. Took a train to Valencia where we spent about two weeks eating tapas. Ran a lot in the Jardí del Túria. Walked on the beach. Flew back to Paris and then straight to New York because we decided to spend the Chinese New Year break there. It was so cold. Took the ferry to Rockaway with Kristen. Visited Chris's grandparents in Connecticut for the day. I organised a surprise birthday party for him even though his birthday wasn't until April. Thirty friends in Niki and Sheila's apartment. We flew back to Paris, then took an overnight bus to Berlin where we sublet Louise's apartment for two months. Maggie came to visit. We did karaoke with Crook and May-Lan. Dinner parties. Abandoned swimming pools. Luna came for a reading. May-Lan had a great party in her new place. I was the DJ and the German metalheads were bemused. The next morning, we took a bus to Prague, spent a few days there. I ran 10km on the first morning. One euro beers, fried cheese. Flew back to Paris again, Notre Dame burned down, then straight to England to see my family. I think we stayed for just over a week, and then flew to Santorini and spent the next two months traveling around Greece.

This year I've been to Paris, once, for two nights in January.

And we took that trip to Marseille and Lyon in February.

We cycled to Decize, a town about 30km away a few weeks ago.

And another day, to Charité-sur-Loire. 25km.

We're currently only allowed to go 10km away from home.

But which year was most ridiculous?

I wanted to start writing while nothing was happening, aside from everything that's always happening. But then Prince Philip died.

'Well, that isn't anything,' Chris said.

'It isn't to you,' I responded sharply.

We were running along the Loire a few hours after the announcement. It's the same old river but the trees along the banks are starting to grow green leaves.

We had decided to go the length of the path that runs about 6km out of the city, and back. My period had just arrived and I was in immense pain throughout but I felt like running if I was going to feel bad regardless.

It's difficult to explain why Prince Philip dying feels like something to somebody who didn't grow up under *The British Empire*, or in England at least. I find myself thinking things like: To you he was just a character in *The Crown*, but to me, he was a character in my whole life.

I'm not saying he was a good character.

Just a part of the archaic furniture.

It makes me think about my grandparents. And especially the two grandads I never really knew. How the world they lived in is slipping away. History is moving forward. I'm moving up a notch.

And I just don't feel ready for any more changes on this Friday afternoon.

My student Jessie submitted some homework. It reads, in part:

'We can play, sing, and dance. That was fun! But we will die and never see the whole world. When I write this sentence, my tears fall down almostly.'

Last time I wrote, women were dying. But now it's men.

DMX.
Prince Philip.
Giancarlo diTrapano.

This doesn't feel any better.

And what a weird list.

I mean, I don't care that Prince Philip is dead. I should probably make that clear. In case you are now under the impression that I'm a big fan of Prince Philip. It's not like that, it's just…

Thinking about when I was 16 and YouTube was a new thing and this guy, Paul Zaleski, played *X Gon' Give It To Ya* on the computer in the art room at school while I painted pictures of the children I babysat, superimposed into a cemetery.

I phoned Grandma to see what she thought.

She didn't have any particularly controversial opinions, just said, 'Poor old Philip, I thought he was a lovely man.' And other things like that.

I felt moved, later, watching a news report on his life.

I felt sad for the Queen.

I felt manipulated.

Maybe this is as close as most English people get to religion.

I always judge people I know who grew up religious and can't quite escape it even when they want to. Or I judge their parents, really. I would never do that to anybody.

But here I am with this weird, hierarchical family existing in the background of my consciousness, connecting me with where I came from, providing a narrative for a nation.

I guess people just want to feel part of something, but I don't like it.

93

We drink red wine with dinner. It's always red wine these days.

We live in Burgundy.

I drunkenly sing along to Amy Winehouse songs on the sofa afterwards and feel like I'm transported back in time.

I think of when I got myself out of my first real relationship when I was 20 and *Tears Dry on Their Own* became the story I told myself.

I think about the 8-track I used to record myself on, how I found it covered in dust at the back of a cupboard at my parents' house last year.

There was an hour-long track of my friend and I playing together for some people at a party in 2009. He was playing guitar and I was singing. Sometimes he was singing too. You could hear all of the background chatter between songs. People making drinks.

I feel like there's a whole story in that.

We haven't spoken to each other in ten years.

But I recorded it!

I have proof that we really knew each other, which I need.

9:55am Saturday morning, cloudy. I slept badly. Kept waking up in pain.

I feel kind of fuzzy, as though hungover.

Where do I start?

Last time I ended up editing for longer than I was writing, so I suppose that if I take the same approach this time, I needn't worry and can just write down anything that I do or think.

What is that again?

I don't really want to spend another week writing about death.

Although this whole period has been marked by it. Obviously.

I should wake Chris up but then the apartment won't be so quiet.

I can stay here like this, a few more seconds.

<u>A list of pleasurable moments since I last wrote to you /
It's not all doom and gloom:</u>

Walking to l'Intermarché to refill the SodaStream canister along the high up path behind the banlieue and telling Chris everything I learned about Proust's teenage sexuality from reading the first chapter of a book called *Proust in Love.*

Talking to May-Lan for four hours after watching the livestream of Gian's funeral. Drinking wine and eating nachos, reliving the history of our friendship out loud.

Swimming in the river on the first day of April. Our whole bodies submerged in cold water. A totem.

Discovering a new supermarket, Grand Frais, on the way home from a long bike ride after our premier halloumi source, Supermarché Nevers Istanbul, had closed early. Rushing into this unknown marketplace twenty minutes before curfew. The look on Chris's face when he found lemongrass and zucchini flowers and galangal. An épicerie du monde in the provinces!

Reading twenty pages of Dennis Cooper's *The Sluts* out loud to Chris on the beach one chilly afternoon. Wondering if the wind was carrying my voice in the direction of a woman sitting not so far away, and if she understood English.

Drinking beers at our homemade beach bar after curfew one evening. We opened the balcony doors and pulled up two chairs and a small table on a rare and warm enough evening with no plans. I played generic beach bar lounge music from my computer and Chris played ocean sounds from his phone. If I closed my eyes it was like I was somewhere.

Running on the other side of the river one sunny afternoon and coming across a field full of sheeps and goats. Hundreds of baby lambs frolicking together, following the mummy sheeps, an occasional billy goat gruff. We stopped to watch them for ages. They were beautiful. Chris said, 'It's so heavenly' and I laughed but then realised he wasn't kidding.

I had a headache all day. I think it's because I have been clenching my jaw. Apparently that's what people do when they are stressed, though I didn't realise I was.

I only managed to go outside for thirty minutes just before curfew. I walked down to the river. Took some photos. The sky was thick and grey. I wasn't listening to anything.

On the way home I saw the perfect present for Chris's birthday in the window of the Faïencerie.

A decorative plate with tiny hand-painted yoga figures on it.

All the shops are closed so I'll have to order it.

9:46am Sunday morning. I could do with a day off. Feels like it should be poetry book club today, but it's next week. Tomorrow I'm talking to Caroline for my new podcast type thing.

If it was a nice morning, I'd like to go running now, but it's not. It's grey and raining. Chris will start a yoga class at eleven. I will teach three long, boring classes.

I planted basil seeds a few days ago.

I'm waiting for them to sprout.

I ordered t-shirts that say ~Profound Experience of Poetry.

I'm waiting for them to arrive.

I just looked up how long it would take to cycle to Illiers-Combray, the town where Proust spent a lot of his childhood. 12 hours, 14 minutes.

Well, originally the town was just called Illiers, but he called his version of it Combray in *Remembrance of Things Past*, and so they decided to change the name on the centenary of his birth, for tourism.

I don't think we'll be cycling there.

It's 230km further away than we are currently allowed to travel.

Chris and I are writing a book together. It's about last summer when we cycled to a park in every arrondissement in Paris to have a drink.

It might be a disaster.

8:11pm. I've just been reading some more of *The Sluts* under a blanket.

And now I'm reading Francisca's manuscript because I'm doing a blurb. It's really good. Her book is called *Hard Summer* and it comes out in June.

I'm thinking about when we met in Lisbon a couple of years ago and she was really young. I don't know how I felt then. About anything, I mean.

Nurturing young writers, especially girls, is really important though.

Monday.

I'm reading the first 16 pages of Caroline's manuscript. It's insane.

I said to Chris, 'She's just better than everybody else.'

I don't understand how she does it.

A few days ago when I was running, I started thinking that I should just move to the US and start a press.

I started picturing it. We would live on Cape Cod and I would spend my time editing, occasionally going into New York to do events, or going on tours.

I could publish all of the books I know about that haven't found homes. I could celebrate those people's works. Those people. I could fuck things up!

When I was running, it felt like a good idea. I started thinking, why haven't I considered what I want to do after all this? What am I going to do with the rest of my youth? There's only so much I can achieve from all the way over here!

But then when I got back home, I looked at Instagram for about twenty seconds and saw the monstrosity of publishing and marketing and America and remembered... No.

I don't want that.

Monday afternoon, we walked around Nevers. We were going to do some kind of substantial grocery shop but then we just decided we didn't want to. Took some streets we'd never walked on before. We sat by the river and I reread the pages Caroline sent to me.

I refreshed whatthefuckshouldimakefordinner.com enough times that it suggested something we could eat. A lemon, feta, basil, tagliatelle. We stopped at the Carrefour City to buy what we needed.

I suggested that Chris should go to a yoga class while I was talking to Caroline so that he wasn't just trapped in the bedroom feeling restless. (He goes to a yoga class at around this time every single day so it was no great inconvenience.)

I guess part of me wanting to do these conversations has to do with Gian dying. (This isn't completely true, because I had already had the idea and conducted one conversation before it happened.) But when he died, May-Lan told me she had just listened to him on *Otherppl*, and Matt wrote that he had relistened to his episode of *Almost Live at Mellow Pages*.

Everybody wanted to hear him speak.

I listened to his *Otherppl* episode the morning after we heard the news. I was running by the river, as always, and it was fairly early, nobody around. The sun was really bright, reflecting off the water. I didn't have a long time, I had to go teach afterwards, but I ran about 7km and as soon as it was over, I barely remembered any of it, felt like I hadn't been there, had floated.

So what am I saying? That I want to record my friends in case they die? In case I do? I mean, as Jessie said, we will never see the whole world.

But I want to shine a light on people.

That's what he did.

Tuesday, 1pm. My student is late and I'm feeling like I can't be bothered. Tuesdays are always my long days lately, I teach seven classes in a row.

We had a nice dinner last night.

We have a nice dinner every night.

Fatigue is setting in. A hundred and twenty something days into the curfew.

The weather is back to being cold.

I'm thinking about cycling to the sea. I look up routes and equipment.

It's 800km, but there is a bike path that runs all the way there along the Loire and it starts here.

There is a line in an old Tao Lin poem that I think of sometimes, something about how no matter how you feel, you'll feel differently in 4 hours.

In the shower, I was thinking about how this is such a nothing week.

It's cloudy and sort of cold every day.

The fact that I had to scroll down to page 15 of this document felt surprising.

Although I guess that's what I was hoping for when I started to write.

Now I can say everything I want to say!

What could I possibly have to say?

Chris and I ran 7km this afternoon. We ran on the other side of the river, the sort of wild side that starts from the beach and acts as a flood plain. I don't know if I'm doing this river justice, but I think I should say, the Loire feels like the Mississippi or something. They call it the last wild river of Europe. The longest river in France. It sort of feels like standing next to the sea, but all rushing by in one direction.

It has felt like the lifeblood of our existence since we moved here in September for the second wave. I keep using the word *feels*.

It feels, it feels, it feels.

This river feels like something powerful.

I wish you could stand next to it.

I wish you could stand in it, with me.

Maybe one day.

Suddenly everything is bright green.

The sheep have gone.

Probably on supermarket shelves by now.

A few nights ago we were sitting on the sofa at the end of another evening, sort of enveloped together beneath a blanket, laughing about something. And I don't know why I said it, but suddenly I realised, 'I know everything is horrible but at least we're happy together.'

It might not sound like much of an assertion to make, but it catapulted Chris out of the moment.

He always has an adverse reaction to somebody stating that things are okay, or that we're lucky for whatever we have. Is that a French thing? I have read articles. Though I still felt a little deflated.

I said it was fine and got up to go to bed, and he stayed on the sofa. I brushed my teeth and collected my electronics. But then he called me back into the room, feeling bad about it, and I rejoined him in the nest. 'I don't want to spoil the evening,' he said, and I just held on to his body and didn't say anything.

'Do you think I'm unhappy or just incapable of admitting I'm happy?'

He started smiling as he said this. As though he had just figured out some eternal problem within himself. And soon we were both laughing again.

But maybe I'm starting to tell his story.

I feel completely detached from the feeling I had a few days ago that it is in any way significant to my life that Prince Philip died. Or perhaps I've just accepted it. There is a sort of processing time, internally, I've noticed lately. The time it takes to categorise somebody from living to not anymore.

Exact wait times vary.

But Prince Philip dying is not the kind of thing that I would ever choose to write about, or even remember. I would just edit it out of my memory, and reaffirm my personal narrative, that I don't give a shit.

Unless I was writing down everything that happened for a week.

Wednesday morning, under a blanket as usual. The sound of the washing machine thrusting itself into the rinse cycle. I am reading Sebastian's book, *Not I*. I will talk with him later for the podcast. It is sunny and I shouldn't have washed my favourite sports bra.

I don't have a class until 12:30 today.

I could fit an extra run in before I teach.

I'll have to wear a backup.

It is genius to go running before you shower.

Then you only have to shower once.

The washing machine beeps loudly to let me know it has finished, I hang up the washing on the drying rack. The clothes horse, as we call it, in England.

I want to use the exact vocabulary I use in my life, whether colloquialisms or borrowed from other languages. I have spent too long trying to assimilate into American literature. Although this isn't of overwhelming concern right now, just something I think about regularly and wanted to share.

For example, in the book that Chris and I are writing, there should be an abundance of French words and phrases, as there are in our every day.

I need to replace the tulips that are dying in the vases.

My basil seeds are yet to sprout.

I ran 5km along the river. Oh my god, it felt amazing. Bright sunshine, the river sparkling in the light. I suddenly felt as though I was in touch with the ancestors. Whose ancestors? Not mine. But you know, the people who lived here before me. Not that they went running or had phones they could play audio from. I listened to Proust for the first half of the run and then when I stopped for a moment to look at the river before turning around, I switched to Fiona Apple. Extraordinary Machine. I, myself, felt like one. I felt like a moving museum curated by me. It is magic to be able to listen to whatever I want to outside in the sunshine for half an hour before I go home to talk to children in China. The ancestors didn't have this. But it is magic to see the sunlight reflected off the water, too.

I ran up the steps from the riverside and when I emerged back on the road, Chris was running towards me. Well, fancy seeing you here.

I asked him, what are you doing? And he said that he'd thought he would join me. Okay but I have a class in thirty minutes, I need to go home! So he said he would run back with me to the apartment, and then continue on his way.

I feel so simple.

As we passed an old, ornate pharmacie building, I looked up and pointed out a small, high up statue to Chris and said, *Straight Outta Combray.*

I laughed at myself.

What I had wanted to do originally this week was to write about this town that we're living in, because we're not allowed to go anywhere else. And I think it's interesting. But I haven't even gotten to the details yet.

I am always trying to communicate with you, and myself in the future.

I know that I'll forget it all, how it really feels.

I would never remember this nothing week.

Except that now I will have to because I wrote it down.

One of my AirPods fell out of my running pouch by the front door when I was returning from the triumphant run.

I found it close by, hours later, crushed by a car.

I enjoyed a great conversation with Sebastian for the podcast.

I feel as though my life has been affirmed.

Thursday again. I will stop writing today.

The sun is coming out again.

I think that by the next time I write to you, it will be warm every day. I wonder if we'll be allowed to go anywhere. The current lockdown restrictions are in place until May 2nd, but it never ends when they say it's going to.

It is rumoured that outdoor terrasses will open in mid-May, but who knows.

It feels impossible.

I make myself feel a little better by planning this potential bicycle trip to the sea. It would take about 9 nights, I think.

Nevers to Cosne-sur-Loire to Gien to Orleans to Blois to Tours to Saumur to Angers to Nantes to Saint-Brevin-les-Pins.

Strangely, we have already been to Saint-Brevin-les-Pins. A tiny town on the Loire-Atlantique coast. We took Bongo there about three years ago. It was just a random place where we could get a cheap Airbnb that accepted dogs.

He loved running on the beach so much.

We loved watching him.

My student Sky told me that he had to run 1000m yesterday in PE class. (He said this as though it was an inordinate distance.)

His school has a 250m track and they had to do four laps. He stopped to walk for a few seconds at the start of the final lap, which slowed his time down. But he completed it.

I tried to give him practical advice about how to improve, which basically just consisted of practice. *It's very tiring but it only takes 5 minutes a day*, I told him. He complained of struggling to get oxygen and I told him that this was what he needed to focus on. I said, *your legs are fine. It's just your lungs. Focus on your breathing.*

I talked about the psychological side of things and how we all want to win.

He said, 'I'm fat, so I know I can't win. I just don't want to be last.'

I didn't really know what to say to that.

We had dinner on zoom with Crook this evening.

Thinking back now to the last time we saw each other in person in Berlin just before Christmas of 2019. We went to a mediocre Vietnamese place in Neukölln. It was great. Each person's meal cost like six euros. We talked about all the projects we were working on and what we were going to do next. We walked together into the cold night for a while afterwards and he got onto the S Bahn. It felt like the end of a long year.

Did we make plans for when we would see each other again?

Probably not. We didn't need to.

Now we see each other all the time.

Dinners, yoga classes, book clubs.

I started trying to explain something while we were on the call. Chris was becoming increasingly bothered with me as the night wore on. It's frustrating, this thing of trying to both cry out at the laptop when everyone starts sharing their fears.

I was trying to explain about how I'm beginning to feel connected to the landscape here.

I had been thinking, on my run, about something Alice Munro said about the area in Ontario where she and her husband live. How she feels like she can never leave.

(I don't feel like that.)

But I'd never really felt close with any landscape before, until last year when we spent the first lockdown, the first spring, in Yorkshire with my family. With nothing to do, and nowhere to go, I started to pay attention to the dirt in the fields and the buds forming in the trees and the slight shift in the light every evening. The slow build of spring felt like a revelatory experience. I had never spent so much time in the countryside.

Chris said something like, you can travel without going anywhere, if you're very patient. The seasons will keep changing. You'll be in a different place.

I think about what we have now and how much it looks like what people have always had. Living in one place, never going too far away, thinking about food and where to find it, longing for things.

I know that I was overstimulated before any of this happened. I couldn't keep up with the pace of life. I didn't want to. I didn't want to make more money so that I could keep up with the people who make more money. I didn't want to know what everybody was doing all of the time and to feel like I should be doing it too. In a sense, hasn't that been a great part of this whole experience, not missing out on anything?

Maybe some people feel they have missed out on everything.

But I haven't.

The ~Profound Experience of Poetry t-shirt arrived in the mail.

And one of my basil plants is beginning to sprout the tiniest little white stem poking out from the soil. The others should follow soon.

Life is moving forward.

Slowly.

Closing thoughts on April 16th as I go to bed?

No. Not really.

I'm tired.

FAVOURITE BOOK

I was invited, by my friend Sebastian, to write something about my favourite books, for a column he edits called 'Favourite Books.'

He told me, 'You can write about these books in whichever manner you feel best suits you.'

I thought about it a lot, every day, as I walked or ran along the river.

What can books do?

And what are they for anyway?

Hi Sebastian,

Thank you for asking me about my favourite books.

I'm going to write about this, as though I am writing only to you, because I don't believe other people are particularly interested in my answer. And I'm going to write, really, only about one book, because this is the book which has most profoundly affected me.

Thirteen summers ago, I was living in Montréal with my best friend Marie-Soleil. We were living this luminous time of trying to figure out how to be adults. And I was reading all of this mid-twentieth century American literature and playing Amy Winehouse songs on my acoustic guitar every day. As you'll remember, it was when we had the internet, but we didn't live here yet. 2008. And I don't think I was aware of the crash, at all. I mean, I know I wasn't. We lived in a bubble made of jazz and frozen pierogies. We drank boxed wine on the balcony and watched the elderly neighbour from across the street come down late at night and reorganise everyone's recycling bins. We rented all of the Disney movies from Blockbuster on DVD and accompanied them with Smartfood popcorn.

I was just about to go into my final year of formal education, and I had finally figured out what I wanted to do: live an interesting life and write books about it. If there were no good jobs, then that felt like a relief, as I had no intention of doing one.

One day I remember we rode our bikes down to the Parc-Jean Drapeau and took it in turns reading out loud from *Howl*. (We had zero sense of self-awareness about this, which I'm glad about.) We were always learning new things and making collages about them. I was always writing songs about love, and how much of a disaster it was. One day I dropped a beer bottle on the floor and slashed my foot open and just let it heal. (I still have the scar.) Mostly we just went to Value Village/Village des Valeurs, to buy ridiculous clothing, or up the mountain to get some perspective.

Marie-Soleil was the person I had been waiting my entire life to meet.

But I should probably begin telling you about my favourite book, as that is what you have asked me to write about.

So it was like every book led me to the next one, following a trail of namedrops. (Imagine Belle from *Beauty and the Beast* but drinking a can of Rockstar). I would come out of the Redpath Library with a stack of ten hardbacks and carry them back to the apartment to sit on the balcony to try to suck out as much information as possible from every story before they were due back. I found this local jazz radio station that we would play all the time, which is funny, but I felt frenetic. I began to read all of the classic books by all of the classic men from *The Beat Generation* because those were the ones I'd heard of, and I liked them to be honest - I just inserted myself and Marie-Soleil into the roles of the always male, main characters. We planned a trip across America. We foraged the sales racks of Urban Outfitters. We laughed at this invisible humour. And then somewhere, amongst it all, it began to happen...

I found my way towards the women and their memoirs. Diane di Prima's *Recollections of My Life as a Woman*, *How I Became Hettie Jones* by Hettie Jones, *Off the Road* by Carolyn Cassady. There is a genre of book that came out of this time which could only be described as women fighting tooth and nail to prove they ever existed, and it felt like the blood in my veins.

I digress...

One day, I came out of the apartment where I had been babysitting some francophone, toddler twins, (basically following them around saying, *Attention! Attention!*) to find, much to my tristesse, that my bike had disappeared.

My beloved Pacer! (That was the name painted on her frame.)

And then I had to walk everywhere and wonder where she had been taken.

This was all only thirteen years ago but I'm seeing it now in some kind of sepia tone.

And I have no choice but to digress even further now...

So, as you're aware, I run a poetry book club, which is - bla bla bla, I won't go into my relationship with poetry. But recently we read a book by Alice Notley, *The Descent of Alette*, which I enjoyed very much, though I'm not calling it one of my favourite books.

I haven't named my favourite book yet, just so we're clear.

I'm building suspense.

But I read and listened to a lot of interviews with Alice Notley during the time that I was reading her, and there was one idea that kept coming up: *'I had no predecessors.'*

Sebastian, I don't know if I can explain to you how insane this makes me feel but I'm going to try. Alice Notley is only forty-four years older than me, and thirteen years younger than my grandma. My grandma who is still alive. No predecessors! No predecessors! An ordinary woman being able to tell her own story, being able to *live* her own story, it's new! I think people forget that. But I don't forget that, because I remember the shock of the lightning when I found my favourite book, and when I found Marie-Soleil, when we found each other.

Now I'm not entirely sure of how to get out of this digression and back onto the main topic as this is my first time ever digressing in such a formal manner. But I suppose I'm just going to chatter my way back into it. I have to tell you how much of a difference it made that Amy Winehouse existed. I know she has nothing to do with books, but it was her voice, her control, her use of language, I mean, her lyrics are so evocative. I wanted to be like her, although I knew I never could be... and I guess it turned out, she couldn't either.

Thirteen summers ago, I was twenty years old, and that's an ideal time to find your favourite books, when you're really ripe for them and everything is new to you. Although for the purpose of writing about this, I reread the one I'm thinking of to check if I had simply been a basic bitch all this time. And it turns out, no... I haven't been. Or my current self agrees with my younger self, at least.

I should explain to you what happened with the bicycle first though, because it's something I would have never expected...

About a week after the disappearance of Pacer, bored of moving at the speed of a pedestrian, I was scrolling through the used-bikes-for-sale listings and I came across an ad by somebody saying they had found a bicycle abandoned behind their building. Respond with a description of yours if it has recently been stolen, they said. So I wrote them an email detailing Pacer. A blue road bike that I had bought from somebody else on craigslist a few months before.

And it was her! Somebody had taken her to Little Italy from the Plateau, a journey of around 5km, and then just discarded her. It didn't occur to me that the person who emailed could have been the thief, or indeed a serial killer, I just went straight up there and collected my bike from some big house. And the person who found it seemed to be very kind. They even appeared to be hosting a dinner party at the time of my arrival. I half hoped for them to invite me in, but they just handed me the bike and I went off into the night, riding all the way downhill without pedalling. So I had a sense, in that moment, that things were really coming together for me.

The book I love is called *Minor Characters* by Joyce Johnson. I first read it that summer. It is a memoir about being a young woman writer in the 1950s. I love it because it gave me the feeling that I had found a predecessor. An example to follow. A roadmap for how it might be possible to live, which is something that everybody needs. And not everybody has yet. The friendship described between Joyce and Elise Cowen made my life with Marie-Soleil feel important, as though we might be interesting enough to write about, as though we mattered.

'I'm in such a hurry at nineteen to finally be the heroine of my own drama. My life fills with the excitement and newness of love. I'm borne up, up, stronger than any bubble, and I know I'll feel this way forever.'

LAISSEZ VOUS BERCER PAR LE BRUIT DES VAGUES

A New Week,
May 2021

Okay I am going to start writing again.

It is the 8th of May and I am in Paris for the first time in four months. My feet feel very tired and warm from walking all the way along the river to Shakespeare & Company to buy the next poetry book club book, *Postcolonial Love Poem* by Natalie Diaz.

Though when we arrived there, after an hour on foot, there was a long queue outside and we didn't bother to stand in it.

There were so many people along the quai.

More people in one afternoon than I have seen in the past two months.

This morning we had our first ever COVID tests.

Our baptêmes as the pharmacist kept saying.

Today is a public holiday - I'm not sure which one, there are so many in May - and most of the testing sites, along with everything else, are closed. But luckily, because we're in the capital, there is still an urgent pharmacie a 5-minute walk away.

We crossed the Pont Bir-Hakeim, waited a few minutes and then a man stuck a swab an unbelievable distance into the back of our heads.

A TV screen playing a relaxing ocean scene above us displayed the caption, *Laissez-vous bercer par le bruit des vagues.*

Let yourself be lulled by the sound of the waves.

A negative test within 72 hours is required in order to fly to America.

We decided, last week, to go there to get vaccinated.

Everybody there is eligible now and even though the borders are closed to the majority of people, we are allowed to enter because Chris is a dual-citizen and I can go with him, because we are married.

The pharmacist advised us to wear socks on the plane because his aunt went to Vietnam in sandals and got a blood clot.

We said, *okay merci...*

I'm listening to the audiobook of *Une Femme* by Annie Ernaux. I told my mum about it too and she's also reading it. The reason I love Annie Ernaux is because her family is like my family. They worked in factories and shops. She was the first in her family to go to university, to be an intellectual, like me.

Just kidding.

Kind of.

Or I'm reminded of Joan Didion:

'I am not in the least an intellectual, which is not to say that when I hear the word "intellectual" I reach for my gun, but only to say that I do not think in abstracts.'

Taking the train from Nevers at 9pm on Thursday was surreal. Walking through the streets after curfew for the first time. Seeing the sunset from the window. The wobbling train and our massive sandwiches packed into a Tupperware because we'd run out of tin foil. Mini bottles of red wine for the journey.

I brought another Tupperware full of my tomato and basil sprouts, which I am leaving in the care of Chris's dad.

Getting on The Metro at Bercy and taking the Line 6 to his parents' apartment...

How it feels to be amongst people again...

After our failed attempt to go to the bookstore, we decided to risk a beer along the river.

We bought cans of Desperados from a Carrefour City and sat beneath Notre Dame and got into an argument about happiness.

Sometimes I just can't believe I'm married to a person called Chris.

What's more surprising? Being married? Or this word 'Chris'?

It was a warm Saturday afternoon and everybody sitting along the Seine had taken their masks off.

People employed by the city collected empty bottles and kept things looking tidy.

It felt sort of civilised.

No sign of the police.

I should mention here, perhaps, that in recent weeks we have seen videos and pictures on social media of the police removing people from the quais by force. Appearing en masse and herding people away like cattle.

But today it feels like things may be edging towards a calmer period.

I took The Metro back to the apartment. I was feeling crazy.

Or my vélib' card wasn't working and my feet hurt too much to walk back.

I stood on the platform at Palais Royal and waited for two minutes as though everything was normal.

Of course, a lot of other people were on The Metro and seemed unperturbed.

I briefly felt like I was the only person who had been living in a pandemic.

Chris taught an online yoga class and then went to an online poetry workshop.

When I was on The Metro, I suddenly had this thought that I could be experiencing the last few days of my pandemic. Maybe when we get back to France in a month, everything will be more relaxed.

I wasn't going to tell anyone we're going but I told Sarah Jean.

LK: i have an insane surprise to tell you

SJ: uh oh

SJ: lol

LK: lol

LK: it's not bad though

LK: i hope

SJ: ??????

SJ: are u pregn

LK: no

LK: lol

SJ: omfg

SJ: i'm die

LK: it's better

LK: we are coming to america

LK: on monday

LK: we are flying to boston

LK: because we can't take this anymore

SJ: ?????????????

SJ: omfg

SJ: MONDAY HAHAHAHHAA

Monday morning, I need to write about yesterday before today happens.

Oh, today started happening already.

I just got an email telling me that my ESTA visa has been cancelled.

I called somebody from immigration services who said, 'Huh?!' at one point while I was speaking.

I'm feeling woozy again. Maybe I always get this feeling during my period but never noticed because I never wrote about it before.

Why am I always writing while I'm bleeding now?

You might get the impression that it's all I ever do.

Yesterday afternoon we met up with Will in the Jardin du Luxembourg.

I cycled there en vélib' and as I passed the Musée d'Orsay, I stopped at traffic lights in the new bike lane and looked to my right on hearing loud music. I saw a group of people practicing the tango in front of the closed museum.

I flashed back to being in Athens a couple of years ago and seeking out this place next to an old train line where people danced the tango on a certain night of the week. How it was this mythical experience to observe in a strange place.

Suddenly today, these people came out of nowhere.

And now, no matter what happens, people say, 'Nature is healing.'

I arrived at the parc ages before Chris because he had gone to his yoga studio in the 10th to talk about translating some yoga book, but I found Will amongst the crowds. Found some green, metal chairs to sit on. We caught up and talked about COVID, talked about our jobs, talked about French people, and Gian and how his passing made us want to do something.

He said this interesting thing about dealing with any kind of international bureaucracy and how he just assumes it's all going to go wrong, which is exactly how I feel any time I have to fill in a form. He said that his new girlfriend (who isn't that new anymore, we just haven't met her because there has been a pandemic), is good at that stuff. She believes that whatever the issue is can probably just be solved by following the instructions.

Imagine.

After a while, Chris arrived and then it started to rain and I proposed that we have a drink somewhere. (I think I'm just using the word proposed here, because *proposer* means *to suggest* in French and I hear it all the time, but I realise that it doesn't sound like a normal way of speaking in English, though I'm going to leave it in.)

We walked to a Franprix and bought beers and then walked to the tables outside of the Pantheon where we had drinks the last time we saw each other, last summer.

We told him we were going to America tomorrow to get vaccinated and I asked him if he had considered doing this too. (He's American.)

He said that because he had been through this whole experience with his girlfriend, he didn't feel like he could leave her now. (She's French.)

I have already had this same conversation with another friend, in another country.

I understand.

We invited them to Nevers, well we offered our apartment to them while we're away, but he said he'd rather wait until we get back so that we can go together.

I hope we can.

Later, at dinner with Chris's parents, I said, *maybe this is it for us!?* Maybe these have been our last days of living under tight restrictions. Maybe things will only get better from here.

But they seemed sceptical, which I felt surprised about. They have always been a lot more confident or optimistic about everything than we have.

But I guess I appreciated the realism.

In the taxi to Orly now.

Going to have to start writing on my phone or I'll forget something.

Crossing the Seine over Pont Grenelle. The Eiffel tower to my left.

Pit of anxiety in my stomach.

I taught two classes just before leaving.

Eden and Carina.

Carina is a pain.

Flights to Lisbon then Boston.

Feeling very nervous at the number of things that could go wrong.

Ran, this morning, to André Citroën. My favourite park.

Will be so relieved if the next thirty hours pass successfully.

On the Peripherique now talking about what Chris should write in the workshop he's taking, coming up with ideas.

I almost forgot what we were doing here for a moment.

Check-in nightmare.

We had to get Another kind of COVID test for our one-hour layover in Lisbon.

They scrutinized our marriage certificate for a long time.

Finally let us check in.

We ran around the airport frantically.

Received our new test results by text at the departure gate.

On the plane now, had a beer and a Xanax.

So stressful!

Oh man.

On the second plane now listening to Amy Winehouse with my headphones plugged into the seat in front.

We had this abstract experience of being in Lisbon for half an hour.

Another round of scrutiny over our documents.

We bought Porto and Vinho Verde and pastéis de nata from duty free.

While we were in the air the first time, my essay about my favourite book was published in Peach Mag.

Francisca messaged me while we were on the runway to tell me she liked it.

And I told her that I was in her city and that I was waving to her.

We flew over Lisbon and pointed out all the places we recognised from above.

I wanted to be there so badly, for it to just be normal.

When we arrived in America, we went through customs together as usual. We watched this insane video of an extremely diverse selection of people smiling maniacally and saying WELCOME repeatedly while we stood in the line.

I whispered to Chris, 'Yeah, welcome in Soviet Union...'

The customs official who dealt with us had a bag of chocolates on his desk called 'Buncha Crunch.'

I kept thinking it, the whole time that he was taking my photo and my fingerprints, 'Buncha crunch.' My life, my health, my freedom are in the hands of someone eating a product called 'Buncha crunch.'

He said that because I was not a citizen and because my ESTA visa had been cancelled, he would need to send us to some secondary person.

A less important seeming man was called to escort us to another location on a different floor. While we were there, we watched a white man who looked like a pig rifle his way through a black couple's suitcases.

As this was happening, they talked with him amiably and laughed at his jokes.

Chris tried to text his brother to tell him we were being held up, but the pig, suddenly noticing us, yelled across the room to tell him to put his phone away.

It started to feel like things were going to get confused and that this man was going to end up going through our suitcases too, because nobody else seemed to be dealing with us. But then after maybe ten or fifteen minutes, another man appeared and escorted us to a third location.

On the way to whatever office we were going to, he informed us that there was no problem and that it was not my fault my ESTA visa had been cancelled. It was, in fact, 'just because of this whole COVID thing.'

When we reached the next room, the original man reappeared and took our passports and marriage certificate again and informed us that he was going to give me a visa waiver form. He said that usually there is a charge for this but that they were going to give it to me for free on this occasion.

I thought this a little rich as I had already paid for the ESTA visa they had cancelled, but I didn't say anything and reacted graciously.

Chris's brother and his boyfriend picked us up at arrivals and we drove to their grandparents' house on Cape Cod, which took about an hour and a half.

On the highway, in the dark, it felt surreal to not only be outside at night but to pass by places like *Taco Bell* and *Panera Bread.*

We arrived after midnight at the house and went straight to sleep.

I got up at 5:30am and taught for three hours.

I told some of my students that I was in America now and that I had taken a plane since I saw them yesterday.

I hadn't wanted to mention it before in case something went wrong.

We pumped up the tires on the old bikes in the garage and cycled thirty minutes along the sea to get to Falmouth to go to Walgreens to get the vaccine.

We had a little time to kill before our appointments, so we stopped on the beach and ate the mozzarella and tomato sandwiches we had bought in Lisbon but failed to eat on the plane.

Sitting in the pre vaccination area at Walgreens.

I really need to go to the bathroom.

We booked appointments online before we arrived.

12:30 and 12:45pm.

I feel nervous about the administration of this.

I'm not bothered by the injection.

I'm armed with the state's guidelines about how nobody is obligated to show identification, in case they question my non-American passport...

I ticked the box on the form that says I do not have health insurance and left the details of my 'primary healthcare provider' blank.

I entered the address of Chris's grandparents' home.

Terrible country music in this Walgreens.

America seems strange and unreal, as usual.

It's an absurd feeling to be able to communicate with people in English.

The pharmacists are shouting out normal things to one another, and I can't believe it, but it is me who is unusual.

The bright sea.

The sound of the waves.

I feel like I'm in a video game.

A quest to cross the ocean to go to Walgreens to have somebody stick a needle in my arm.

This is the final obstacle!

If these people only knew what we have been through to get here...

Am I going to break down from the sheer relief?

As I type, I just feel insane, like I've forgotten why we are doing this.

Momentarily we will be called into what appears to be a closet and from then on, our lives will be changed.

We did it.

I fell off my bike on the way back to the house, my wheel got stuck in some sand on the side of the road and I tipped over slowly, fell into a pile of soft sand. No problem.

Getting the vaccine was so easy. They didn't even ask for ID.

Kind of anticlimactic.

Lying on the bed on Tuesday afternoon.

I can't stop thinking about the disparity between here and France and the rest of the world.

It doesn't feel fair.

Because it isn't.

We asked the pharmacist, 'Aren't we supposed to wait for 15 minutes to see if we're okay?'

She said, 'Yes, but you can shop while you wait!'

Quel horreur.

Picked up some shampoo and toothpaste though.

Felt a strong and terrible feeling of having left people behind.

Cooking dinner in the house.

Chris's brother and his boyfriend went to the gym.

I guess gyms are open here...

I felt really tired after getting home from the vaccine appointment but that might have just been because I'm really tired.

No other side effects so far.

My computer says 2:03am but I suppose it's really 8 o'clock here.

If I woke up tomorrow and was back in Nevers, that would make more sense to me.

But if I wake up here again, I will try to write in full sentences.

4:41am. Can't sleep. Fifty minutes until I need to get up to teach. I wanted to write something. Typing on my phone in the dark, birds are chirping wildly outside.

Yesterday we saw a yellow one and Chris said it was a goldfinch, but I think he was just saying things.

My arm feels heavy and sore, but I feel fine otherwise.

I'm worrying about a friend and her experience publishing her book.

Just looked up through the skylight and saw a tiny light moving across the sky, way up in the distance. Strange to think there are people there.

I can't believe I was in a plane two days ago after a year and a half without flying. I have to completely dissociate from the experience, not think about what's really happening at all.

Chris just sighed deeply. A few minutes ago he asked me if I was alright and I said yes and he said I should try to sleep more.

So tired today.

17:22.

We clambered on some rocks for a long time and now we're sitting on a bench on someone's private beach.

Thinking about Nevers and the Loire.

Wondering how our plants are doing.

9:19am.

I keep forgetting what I'm doing.

I'm trying to order food to be delivered from *Stop 'n' Shop.*

Everything is extremely expensive, relative to what I'm used to.

Can't decide whether to order firm tofu or extra firm tofu...

Clicked extra firm and then imagined it and removed it...

Then clicked firm...

Doesn't feel right either......

Thursday now. I felt like I was crashing all of yesterday. Drowsy and woozy all day long.

Today it was a little more difficult to get out of bed, but since then I have felt fine.

This morning, Chris and I went running on the route that I used to do last time we were here. It felt strange to realise that Chris had never done it with me before. We ran to the lighthouse and then went to sit on the rocks. We talked about a stressful family issue that I don't think I should write about here.

We talked about a publishing problem a friend is having.

We kept rolling our eyes about *the discourse*.

We decided that everyone's problem is that they are all too deeply involved in society...

Whereas we don't really exist.

Everything that happens...

To everyone we know...

We seem to witness from outside of their culture...

I quite like it.

5:32pm. I have just been swimming in the ocean for a few minutes.

I feel kind of like my body is restarting.

Everybody has been saying the water is too cold to swim in (admittedly, it is 9°C) but Chris's brother saw someone doing it yesterday, so I wanted to try too.

And to be honest, it didn't feel that bad. I think our multiple times swimming in the river in April were good training. I just walked right in and started swimming after a few seconds.

Chris was really hesitating and taking his time getting in but eventually he did it too.

Now he's upside down on his head in the middle of the living room and we're waiting for *Stop 'n' Shop* to deliver our groceries.

Had a sort of awkward conversation about different places in Europe with a local man who stopped us in the bakery after hearing my accent. He kept talking about his travels to London and Barcelona and telling us about how cultural Barcelona is.

I don't know what he meant by that really, but I kept thinking, does this man seriously think we've never been to Barcelona?

On the one hand, he's using us as a sounding board to reminisce about his experiences, because we're from Europe... On the other hand, he's trying to explain Europe to us?

People are awkward, people keep saying. You have to give people a little slack, etc. To be honest, in every conversation I've been part of since we arrived (just a handful), I have found myself floating slightly above myself thinking about how I could get out of the situation, watching people play out the roles they've assigned themselves.

Really feels like a lot of people are just playing a character, to me, right now. I want to say, come on, you're not really like that, are you?

The woman in Walgreens who was too excited about every single thing we did or said. 'Wow! You came here on bikes! That's awesome!'

I mean, why are you doing that?

It makes me want to cry.

At the supermarket we visited right after getting vaccinated there were two women serving us. Well, you know how it is in America sometimes, there is the one person who processes the order and handles the money and then the other person who, for no apparent reason, puts your things into a bag for you.

We told the bagging lady that we didn't want her paper bag because we had brought our backpacks and would be cycling home, so she took great pains to place every item into our bags and comment on each of them.

I mean...

I have a tab open, 8 Benefits of Cold Water Swimming.

One of them is 'increased libido.'

We're on the sofa now, after dinner. Chris is translating a Belgian TV show about some people training for the Paralympics, or something.

I finished listening to *Une Femme*, or as it is called in English, *A Woman's Story*. It was a great book. I really enjoyed it. Made me feel sad and miss my nana.

Drinking wine from the box again.

I guess being here, in some ways, makes me realise how much I love living in France. The *mode de vie* just feels more compatible with me.

I mean this town isn't really America. We could be anywhere, most of the time. We're just in a house in a forest by the sea.

But it freaks me out how long it takes the vegetables to rot here.

<u>A list of things I should maybe explain or at least mention:</u>

What's the deal with this empty house...

Why I chose to write about this week of activity after the previous week when nothing happened...

I guess that's just common sense...

How my teaching schedule remains on Beijing time so I now have to wake up at 5:30 every morning...

I guess whatever happens in the next couple of days of writing is going to feel anticlimactic after the drama of the first few days. I hope so anyway. It's been a week now since we left Nevers, but it doesn't feel like what's happened could really be measured in time.

I just did a word count and I have written just over two and a half thousand words this week. I thought it was more like a thousand. What am I going to do with this project? How long will it go on for?

I would like to collate it all and call it Troisième Vague, or Third Wave, I think.

I read somewhere that in a series of ocean waves, the third one is always the strongest.

Saturday morning. I'm back in bed after teaching. I don't feel so good. Maybe a little hungover, though I went to bed at 10:30pm.

Our friend Henry arrived from New York.

Chris and I made pizzas and patatas bravas and a big salad.

First time cooking for other people in a long time.

I felt awkward, at first, seeing Henry but it quickly began to feel normal.

Until after dinner, when two girls appeared at the door.

Friends of Chris's brother and his boyfriend.

I was shocked!

I felt so uncomfortable. They just walked into the house and then one of them came and sat next to me on the sofa, unmasked. I was thinking, what the fuck!!!

I felt upset that nobody had warned me about more people coming.

Annoyed that the conversation was suddenly like, *How do you all know each other?* rather than catching up.

Everything is so different here.

Or I mean, I just haven't been around anybody new in a year and a half.

I went to bed feeling stressed.

I'm actually writing about Saturday on Sunday morning, so I'm running over by a day but it was a busy day and I need to tell you about it now before I move on.

In the morning, Chris taught a yoga class outside in the park for his brother and Henry and another neighbour friend. And I decided to go too, because I wanted to be a part of things and felt like if I didn't go it would be like I was just making a thing out of not going. I had never done yoga before.

We didn't have yoga mats so we set out beach towels on the grass and Chris played music on the mini-speaker and we went through the class. I found myself having a hard time with it. (Not especially with the movement part, though I did really dislike any time I needed to rest my weight on my arms. That hurt!) But really I just don't like the whole ritual of it. I don't like the tone. I don't like the way it feels preachy. I found myself getting angry while it was happening. I didn't put my hands 'into prayer'. I felt like I was just waiting for it all to be over.

Everybody else seemed to like it though.

There was one part about three quarters of the way through where I started thinking, okay it's not so bad. It's nearly over, I can do this. But then I got angry again at the end when we were supposed to just lie down. I felt agitated and like my skin was burning in the sun so I reached over and grabbed the sunscreen and applied it to my arms and shoulders while everybody lay down with their eyes closed.

I mean, Chris is not a spiritual leader. I mean, I hope he's not. I don't need him to tell me to lie down on the ground with my eyes closed. I don't want anybody to tell me to do that.

Anyway, it was okay. Just an hour of my life.

And the others were happy.

It's just not for me.

Afterwards we came back to the house and I made grilled cheese sandwiches for me and Chris and then he went to his online poetry workshop.

I wrote in here for a while and wrote some emails, sitting on the bed.

Later, Luke and Henry and I decided to take their grandpa's old fishing boat down to the water. It was the first time anybody had touched the boat in years, since their grandpa is ninety-nine years old and can't come to the house anymore.

I put on my white cotton dress and the boys put on shirts with their swimming shorts. Chris came too once he was finished with poems and rowed us out into the bay and we looked back at the beach from this new perspective.

We got married on this beach.

A few years ago now.

We should have had someone taking photos from this angle.

On the water, we drank pink gin cocktails from plastic cups.

At one point, Luke stood up and rocked the boat and everybody screamed against a perfect blue backdrop.

I felt for a moment like I was in that scene at the end of *The Truman Show*.

I swam briefly just to feel the cold.

And then around 7:30pm we all headed back to the house, showered and walked into town to the taqueria.

We ordered burritos and sat outside at a big table and drank beers and dipped chips into guacamole.

The first time I've eaten at a restaurant in eight months.

The moonlight and the sparkling lights, and everybody happy from sun and sea air.

It all just takes some getting used to.

I looked over at The Landfall, a pub across the street and saw some waspy people sauntering out and suddenly felt brimming with rage that any of us could be doing this, knowing that there are so many parts of the world that don't have access to vaccines, so many people suffering.

I can't relax.

But restaurants will open for outdoor dining in France this week too, for the first time since last October. And they're relaxing the curfew from 7 to 9pm.

When we got back to the house everybody looked at all the photos they had taken earlier and said it was the best day they had had in a long time.

I went to bed at 10:30pm as usual, because I need to start teaching at six.

APRÈS TOUT, OUI

A week is a long time,
June 2021

It's Wednesday June 16th and I'm writing again. I just woke up in Paris for the first time in five weeks. We arrived back from America yesterday afternoon and now we're housesitting for Chris's parents while they're away visiting family.

My body feels like it's been hit by a ton of bricks. Like it's run out of battery. Jet lag going in this direction is miserable. My muscles ache.

But I'm so happy to be here.

I have to teach a class in an hour, which feels ambitious.

Hopefully this week will be uneventful and I can write about everything that has happened in the past month.

Don't I always say that?

I'm astounded by how many place-specific pieces of information my brain can remember. Like that the clock on the oven at Chris's parents' apartment is a few minutes fast. Or that the 'A' train runs local stops at night except from 59th to 125th street. Or that the bakery on Rue de Passy is closed on Tuesdays. Recycling goes out every other Monday on the Cape, etc...

But I still struggle to grasp the rhythms of the tides in accordance with the moon, which is what I really want to remember...

I talked to Caroline on zoom for three hours about my time in the US, her recent break up, and the future of the poetry book club.

It felt just as real as anything, although she was inside of my computer.

Now Chris wants me to go to the 18th to meet him and some yoga friends somewhere.

But I need life to slow down again so I can write to you about it!

Ahhh. Amazing news! The government has just announced the end of the wearing-masks-outside mandate from tomorrow. Oh my god, I'm so happy.

And the 11pm curfew is ending early! From Sunday! What a relief!

Our timing is perfect.

I can't believe it's really changing here...

Finally.

I tried to give Caroline a kind of pep-talk about being open to new experiences and how there is this enormous potential for joy going forward.

I need to take my own advice too.

Since we got back to Paris I've been feeling overwhelmed with happiness, just seeing people *en terrasse* and shops being open. It feels unbelievable to see that life has returned to the streets.

(How a scene changes so fast.)

But what is my life going to be like?

I have a break between classes and I wanted to write something. My body still feels strange, like it doesn't need to perform all its functions. Eating, for example, is superfluous.

I feel this sudden acceleration of time. Things are actually happening again and I haven't had the chance to process whatever happened in America at all.

I feel torn between going outside and experiencing the world, and staying here, sitting with the past few weeks, and trying to hold onto what it all means to me.

<u>Maybe I need to keep a list of moments I want to
remember:</u>

Talking with Sarah Jean on the sofa on Friday night.
Laughing more than I have in two years while pretending
to be crabs, for some reason.

Talking with Rachelle on the beach about our families and
feeling our friendship deepening in real time.

Dancing like crazy at 2am with Jake and Niki and Chris
and Sarah Jean and Jordan and Brooke. Going so hard for
so long and never wanting it to end.

Hanging out on Peter's rooftop and going downstairs to
his apartment for a screening of the film he made during
the past year. Feeling so inspired and impressed and
proud of him.

Going into the bathroom to cry by myself after dancing to
Beyoncé with Sarah Jean and Kristen.

How we all had tears in our eyes as we walked to the
subway.

The dinner with Liz and Will at their apartment, meeting their dog and falling into our own little symposium.

Singing *If I Had A Million Dollars* as a duet with Chris when we did karaoke in the house and realising that our friends watching were becoming emotional.

Driving to the airport with Niki and Sheila and making plans for the future for the first time in forever.

Watching the sunset again and again after not seeing it go down in so many months and simply not being able to believe it.

How do I write this?

I think this will be the last time I write to you.

But does that mean I have to say it all now?

I had this experience a few weeks ago, I was running in Central Park and I was thinking about all these things I have written and what I'm trying to do. I don't know what this kind of writing is, or how it fits together.

But I want to write many short books, like Annie Ernaux.

I want to use what I wrote about Joyce Johnson as a reminder to myself that living the life that I want to live and writing it down *is* worth sharing with other people.

Last night, I cycled over to the 18th to meet Chris and some of his yoga friends in someone's backyard. The bike ride took me around 35 minutes and it felt strange to suddenly be back in the Paris heat navigating the dry streets *en vélib'*. I didn't arrive until almost 10 o'clock, but of course it was still bright daylight.

The four people present in the little garden were all speaking French, which I had only half-anticipated because I thought that many of the people Chris does yoga with at the studio were anglophone. It was okay, or I mean I could understand what people were saying. But I found that when I opened my mouth to respond, I couldn't find the words to make sentences. I used the excuse of jetlag and having spent five weeks in America, not thinking in French. But the truth is that really I have spent a year and a half not speaking to anybody. I've been reading things and listening to things in French the whole time, but when was the last time I was part of a group conversation in that language? I can't remember.

The girl who lived there moved across the garden to sit next to me and we kept switching back and forth between the two languages. I found it easier speaking to just one person, but also frustrated with myself and the slow pace at which I could conjugate verbs in my head before speaking them. I could hear myself making mistakes and that felt unfortunate, but then I could hear her making mistakes too, and of course, I didn't care and could understand her.

There was a man there who was American but seemed to be speaking with an affected, generally European accent, and I started to have the feeling I get when I'm around a male feminist.

Reject! Reject! Reject!

My arms feel tired. My whole body feels exhausted. I haven't been running in days and since returning to Paris have only left the apartment a few times to get supplies, and that one trip over to the 18th. I mean, it's only been three days, but I feel like I'm in recovery. That last weekend in America was really intense.

I was thinking of going running, but it's been over 30 degrees since we got here and I have barely eaten. I went to Castorama to get some vessels to repot my tomato sprouts into, (get yourself a father-in-law who can nurture your plants) but they didn't have anything that wasn't grey so I'm going to order some colourful ones.

And then I went to Franprix to get some yoghurts and Desperados and rosé and when I came back into the building, there was a woman coming in at the same time, pushing a stroller, so I walked up the five flights of stairs, and I felt weak! I don't think I should go running after all.

I probably just need to let myself rest until tomorrow.

And eat some food.

Chris's grandpa is in hospital, again.

We just got a message in the family group chat.

It's difficult because we had wanted to go and visit him while we were in America but because we were only 'half-vaccinated' at that point, we weren't allowed to.

Now, Chris is stomping around the house making a lot of exasperated noises and I'm yelling, 'Well, don't be a bitch to me about it!'

I need to write about the experience of being comfortable around friends before I forget it all.

How does it already feel so far away on Thursday night when I said goodbye to them on Monday morning?

What is it that I need to say?

How it feeds me?

I think that I am a strong person, in that I *can* go without. I have been without these relationships in my life, for most of my life. I didn't always have good friends, and I didn't even meet any of these people until I was 24 years old. But to let people in and stop being resilient... That's really something different.

Up late, drunk, and thinking about this Dennis Cooper quote that Blake Butler tweeted and I can't attribute to a source, so maybe he just said it in a conversation, I don't know:

If you get some power, spread it around.

What I feel about Sarah Jean is so powerful. I can't believe she wants to be friends with me. Best friends. Her support, and the recognition I receive from her, means more than anything else I could describe. I'm so lucky.

Oh dear. I woke up around six to an email from Chris's mom which basically said that his Grandpa is dying and that if he wants to, Chris should go back there now. But he doesn't have to. It's up to him.

I don't really think I should be writing about this.

Oh I just heard him moving around. He must know too.

He got up and came through to the living room where I was sitting and we had a brief conversation about the email and he asked what I thought he should do and I said I didn't know.

I relayed some information I had just read about how long it takes somebody to die once they reach a certain stage of the process.

(I spent a lot of time reading about this last year when my Nana was dying too. My browser remembered the websites.)

I told him various flight prices.

We laughed at the prospect of going back through Lisbon airport on another layover... three days after we were just there.

I guess we're not even discussing the prospect of me going with him.

I don't know.

He's gone back to bed now. It's 8:28 in the morning.

And this is all too personal for me to write about.

I think I might go for a run before it gets too hot outside.

231

12:24pm, I was just sitting here waiting for my class to start in a few minutes and thinking, what am I supposed to be doing? I didn't want to look at anything on the internet. And then I remembered I'm supposed to be writing. I feel very scattered.

I did go for a run along the river. 5km towards André Citroën, which is my usual short run when I'm here, but then when I got close again, I didn't feel like coming back to reality, so I did another couple of kilometres in the other direction.

Chris spent the entire day seemingly believing that he was going to fly back to America tomorrow. But then he taught his first official in-person yoga class and went for drinks afterwards with people from the studio? And I texted him... Are you still leaving tomorrow?

It's 7pm and he doesn't have a ticket but he says he thinks so, yes.

I can just feel that this evening is going to end in disaster. For some reason we are continuing with our original plan, which was to go and watch England play Scotland in the Euro Cup at a bar in the 20th arrondissement.

At the bar, we sat with a random English stranger who was incredibly posh and said he worked for the government and had just been in Monaco. We arrived a few minutes after kick-off and there was no space left at the table with our friends so this person let us join him on the table next to them, and then we had to make small talk.

I felt self-consciously cosmopolitan discussing our lives in Paris and our recent trip to New York or whatever. As though I needed a caveat:

It's not usually like this...

(It used to be though.)

It was good to see Will and meet his girlfriend and to hear they had managed to find vaccine appointments after spending hours refreshing the doctolib website.

At some point, Chris accepted that he's not going to fly tomorrow.

I mean, it was a little far-fetched.

Everybody was talking about how different things feel now and how much pleasure we're getting out of life all of a sudden.

'Everything is fun right now!' I remember exclaiming.

But later we had an argument on the way home.

It's just what happens if we drink and don't eat.

237

We had ordered a vegetarian sharing platter of some kind at the bar but then after a while, when it hadn't arrived and we enquired, the waiter, maybe owner of the bar, not the person who had taken the order, indignantly responded that they didn't have any of those left... Well, we ordered it ages ago, we said, surprised by this... and he retorted, essentially, that this was our problem. It was too late.

Last few days of the now 11pm curfew.

There is a huge thunderstorm outside.

It is 17:59 the next day, Saturday.

I started typing Sunday but stopped myself before I got to the end of the word.

We spent the day in bed together, before and after I taught.

Recovering from jetlag, recovering from last night.

Death often makes people feel sexy, I've noticed.

We spoke to Chris's family on FaceTime.

At one point his mom looked around the room she was in and explained, in French, switching languages, that if Chris does make it there soon, it would probably be for the funeral rather than to say goodbye.

Now the clouds outside are moving really quickly.

Maybe I'm suddenly going to be here alone.

Yeah, I guess I am.

Chris is going back to the US tomorrow. He's leaving at 6:45am.

He just booked a flight.

We had a lot of conversations today about our relationship.

The future.

We had a nice dinner, as usual.

I guess that once I'm alone, I'll be able to write down everything about how I feel, or whatever.

Although none of it feels relevant anymore.

Oh my god.

His sister just phoned and told us that their grandfather
has died.

242

This is a rollercoaster.

Chris is on the phone trying to cancel his flight.

And suddenly everything seemed really funny.

To me. I don't know why.

I had to go and hide in the kitchen to stop myself from laughing at the absurdity of the situation.

A certain kind of shock.

This is our third grandparent death in three years.

His dad's mom, then my mum's mum, now his mom's dad.

Now it's nearly 1am and Chris is just working again. I'm typing in here. He never notices when I'm writing these things. I just tell him at the end of the week, and he seems surprised. I don't know what he thinks I'm doing.

He was able to cancel his flight and get a refund.

The ticket was only booked for around two hours.

He just showed me a clip from the film that he's translating, and it was funny. Some Québécois romantic comedy.

We're drinking red Sancerre that we bought as a gift for someone a few weeks ago and just decided to keep for ourselves instead.

I wonder how we will sleep tonight.

Something about this death is not hitting us that hard.

Chris seems relatively okay.

But then his grandpa was literally ninety-nine years old.

How much more can you get out of life?

There's this mental divide now that didn't exist before.

It felt like I had to break down barriers in my mind in order to be able to enter America and exist among the people we know there and the reality they're living in, and then I had to reconstruct something in order to come back here.

It felt, to me, when we said goodbye to our friends, that it was possible we might not see them again for two more years, or something untold. I made myself begin adjusting back to the idea of life in France a few weeks before we were due to return.

And so the idea that Chris was going to somehow just turn right around and go back there... it seemed incomprehensible to me. The country that we left five days ago would not be an easy place to re-enter. For me anyway. I have to exist, mentally, here now. Does this make any sense?

I didn't feel this before.

I'm so relieved he doesn't have to wake up at 6am and go to the airport.

Maybe he will have to go there soon.

But for now, it feels like we just got our summer back.

Though I suppose it's going to be a different kind of summer.

Sunday. 14:53. Just finished teaching for the day.
Tired and warm. Writing my students' assessments.

16:50.

I walked Chris to a yoga class along the quai. Then I went to the book shop at the Palais de Tokyo. Wandered around thinking about my own book.

I mentioned it to Chris yesterday and he said, *what book?!* And I said *my collected works*.

Now I'm in the gardens of the fashion museum, which were closed for refurbishment for a long time, so I wanted to take the opportunity to walk through the gate.

It's hot again. Actually, it's supposed to storm, so maybe I should head back. I need to plan for the planning meeting we're having for the poetry book club tonight.

I am so relieved that Chris is still here.

Wondering if we both seem to feel okay with this death simply because he was so old, or so far away, or if it's because there is such a sense of moving forward right now. Maybe it feels okay that someone who was almost a hundred years old can't come with us into the next phase of history.

Or maybe we're completely numb.

Though at the same time, everything feels so intense. Like too much at once. Just being out on the street without worrying or feeling scared... I don't know how to process all of it.

I walked home listening to *Just Like Heaven* by The Cure with tears in my eyes because I felt so happy.

You

Soft and only

You

Lost and lonely

You

Strange as angels

Dancing in the deepest oceans

Twisting in the water

You're just like a dream

You're just like a dream

What am I even trying to remember about being in the US that I wanted to write down? It feels impossible to remember.

Though I'm still getting notifications to tell me about great white shark sightings off the coast of Cape Cod.

May-Lan sent me some voice notes because she hurt her wrist and can't type. It sounds as though things feel the same in Berlin as they do here.

I can't wait to go and visit.

I phoned my grandma because it's her birthday.

88 years young.

She seemed happier than she had been in a while, but she couldn't talk for long because her shopping was being delivered.

Monday, 16:03.

Hungover today. We went out last night for *Fête de la Musique*. Although there was little music. We met up with Ida, a Swedish writer who wrote some amazing essays I published in the Quaranzine during the first wave.

Wednesday morning suddenly. Well, no, it's early Wednesday afternoon. The past couple of days went by in a hungover whir. We went out with Ida and her boyfriend in the 10th on Monday night. Didn't have a real meal, ordered too much wine, but it was a fun evening. Everything seems super cheap in comparison with American prices, even in Paris. My French is starting to come back, I think. I'm feeling more confident.

I forgot to mention we went to the Pompidou on Monday afternoon and wandered around the various bookshops inside and went up the escalators to see the view of the city from up high. Though we didn't bother going to see the *Women in Abstraction* exhibition. I didn't feel any desire to. To be honest, everything we do feels like an exhibit now. Walking through the Marais, sitting by the canal, going to the Post Office and sending a postcard to Chris's nana that says, *sorry for your loss.*

The heat wave finally died down and now it rains every afternoon. Thunder and lightning for days.

On Monday, we sat by the canal and drank rosé and ate caviar d'aubergine with these people we only knew from the internet and meanwhile, to my left, a big parade of drummers went by.

Last night we met up with another friend, Yaël. In fact, she is Chris's friend and I had never met her before in person, although she has been coming to the poetry book club sometimes since last autumn.

We met at the Comptoir Moderne in the 15th and had beers and talked about reading and publishing and what languages everybody could speak and who they used them with. Yaël speaks English with her boyfriend and it's neither of their native language. It was the same for Ida and Aviv the night before.

We came back to the apartment and ate pizza and watched the England vs Czech football match. The final group-stage game in the Euros. We talked about Yaël's cousin's wedding which she is dreading.

I'm torn between going running before I start teaching soon and trying to write an emphatic final paragraph to this project. I keep looking up train tickets to Nevers. I want to go there in the next few days to get some more clothes and check if the apartment is alright.

Okay, I decided to go running *after* teaching and I just won't shower before. Who cares?

Qui sait?

I guess the thing I want to say, or the thing that I'm really struck by is just how much easier life feels suddenly. When you don't have to be at home before 7pm and when you can stop to buy food at a cafe because you're on the other side of the city, and you can even use the bathroom while you're there. You can meet up with People! And have long and engaging conversations that meander and go wherever you want them to.

And even with a death in the family, there is comfort in knowing there will be a ceremony with people to ritualise his passing.

And hugging.

I have been enjoying staying in bed for longer than I normally would in the mornings, because I know that my day won't end before it gets dark.

Though I guess we really don't know what's going to happen next and how long this will last for.

By the way, today is the day that I am finally considered 'fully vaccinated.'

There are currently around two thousand new cases of COVID in the country every day. Down from the high of eighty six thousand a few months ago.

What am I going to do?

Finish putting this manuscript together, first of all.

And then we will move into a new phase of life, filled with art and people.

What about you?

Notes on the Titles

The titles for most of these letters came from language I 'found' outside during the times I was writing and editing:

Je veux vivre avec toi or *I want to live with you,* I saw graffitied in an alleyway by the town hall in Lyon on a sunny day in February.

Je ne suis pas seul, il y a les mots or *I am not alone, there are words,* I saw printed on the side of an abandoned building by the train station in Charité-sur-Loire in March.

Straight Outta Combray is something I thought when I was thinking a lot about Proust in April.

Laissez-vous bercer par le bruit des vagues or *Let yourself be lulled by the sound of the waves* was displayed on a TV monitor in a pharmacy in May.

Après tout, oui or *After all, yes* was graffitied on a wall on Rue des Vignes in Paris in June.

Last Call is the final song on the Kanye West record, *The College Dropout*. A 12-minute 40-second track consisting almostly of a spoken-word monologue about how he made the album.

LAST
CALL

(Épilogue)

**'It's impossible to be a modern person
and have any idea what your life is like
unless you know French poetry'**

- **Frank O'Hara**

He said this in a documentary I watched on YouTube about the New York School.

I watched it while I was researching John Ashbery when we were reading one of his books in the poetry book club.

You didn't think I was going to write an entire book without mentioning Frank O'Hara, did you?

I decided not to use the quote as an epigraph because it's insane, (albeit hilarious), and while I cannot say I know French poetry, in any traditional sense, the phrase has stayed with me anyway.

It's impossible to be a modern person and have any idea what your life is like...

I think I agree with that.

But this book is an attempt at understanding.

And it exists because of a whole community of friends and writers.

When I started writing these letters, I had no intention of making a book. I just wanted to communicate with a few specific people. And it was on that run around the Presqu'île in Lyon that I started to imagine a format that might let me do that.

I can recall, vividly, running along the quai and beginning to find these words. Writing them down felt possible, suddenly.

I had been thinking about my friend Matt Nelson's *Lapsed Librarian* newsletter that he writes about the books he reads and how I really appreciate any time he slips in some personal information, some insight into his emotional state. I thought that maybe I could do something like that. Or it gave me this idea that I could write a newsletter without any news. An email you didn't have to respond to.

On March 10th of this year, Caroline Rayner tweeted,

'I want to write a book my friends will like
I don't care about anything else'

And I knew she was right and I agreed with her too.

It makes me think of the *Personism* manifesto, 'The poem is at last between two persons instead of two pages.'

But I didn't want to write to just one person.

I had the internet and I hadn't seen anybody in over a year.

One great thing about having been publishing writing for a decade is that all my friends are writers now, so when I emailed them out of the blue with thousands of words of prose about my day-to-day life, they didn't ask me if I was okay, or if I needed help. They just gave me feedback on the writing, encouraged me to keep on going.

Matthew Bookin wrote, 'It made me feel less alone and less insane as a person who already feels kind of detached or off-center from the world. It made me feel like writing, too.'

Sebastian Castillo wrote, 'Sorry if I'm imposing my desires here, but this, along with what you've written lately, feels like it should be a book one day. I would love to read that book. Perhaps you have other plans—but it's a book I would love to see in the world.'

Maggie Lee wrote, 'I feel incapable of not writing back when you send these, because they are one of the few things I get via the internet that feels like a happy interaction of sorts rather than a stressful one. Really does trigger something chemical in my brain, I feel different when reading this. Like I'm in different places, with people I love, in a different time, not sure if past or future. Which is weird because you're describing a very present time. I don't know. Most of the time lately I feel like I'm in a terrible time and strange not-home place (with someone who makes me happy nonetheless), and that eventually our lives will shift into some other gear, one that I think I'm imagining feels similar to what I feel when I read these. Like, closer to things that feel like home.'

Karina Briski wrote, 'It felt like the best alternative to talking about how shitty everything is. I feel like a lot of people only talk about the shittiness because they feel like they're supposed to. I also feel like this is unique to our socially mediated era. What have people throughout history talked about during wars, famines, pandemics? Certainly, they talked about everything. Living included.'

Stacey Teague wrote, 'I liked seeing the little snapshot of your life. The bit about you and Chris never being able to understand each other. Because maybe two people never really can properly.'

Kristen Felicetti wrote, 'I can say with confidence, 'This is the news we need."

I'm trying to say this book was written in collaboration.

And this epilogue is my acknowledgments.

Thank you to everybody who read these letters as I wrote them.

And thank you to Alina, Lydia, Barbie, Eden, Sky, Grace, Joy, Amy, Jason, Jack, Jessie...

Wǒ de xiǎopéngyǒumen.

This book also came from:

The anticipation of sharing each document with Sarah
Jean after a week of writing and longer editing. Waking
up to her comments and breathing a sigh of relief that
somebody understands.

Reading every letter out loud to Chris (aka Oscar d'Artois)
as we were walking by the Loire or the Seine or when he
was cooking. His facial expressions and reactions making
for the finest editor.

Sebastian challenging me to write about my favourite
book and challenging me to write this one too.

Rachelle publishing the Favourite Books piece in Peach
Mag.

Everybody who reads Minor Characters as a result.

May-Lan listening to me talk this through again and again
and encouraging me / all the nights we stayed up too late
laughing.

Crook responding sincerely and every zoom dinner together.

The poetry book club!

And everybody who was a part of the Quaranzine.

Amy Winehouse. Joyce Johnson. Beyoncé...

La Nièvre.

If you liked this book, look up all the people I've mentioned and read their work too.

We all lived through these waves together.

And I want to tell you something. 12:47am, August 1st, 2021:

I'm really trying to just do things, even if I can't do them perfectly.

Thank you for reading this book.

I'm going to buy myself a new guitar with the royalties.

Lucy K Shaw is the author of The Motion, WAVES, How to Be a Perfect Bride, and Troisième Vague...

She founded the online arts & literature magazines, *Shabby Doll House* and *~Profound Experience* and runs the *~Profound Experience of Poetry Book Club*, which you are welcome to join if you want to.

Shabby Doll House, the online literary magazine (est. 2012), has published hundreds of artists and writers from all over the world.

Shabby Doll House, the publishing house (est. 2021), has published two books, and you just finished one of them. If you enjoyed it, please tell your friends. We hope to make some more soon.

For behind-the-scenes bonus content, visit:
shabbydollhouse.com/linernotes